Colville's People

BOOKS BY CAROL MALYON

fiction
The Adultery Handbook 1999
Mixed-up Grandmas (for children) 1998
Lovers & Other Strangers 1996
If I Knew I'd Tell You 1993
The Edge of the World 1991

poetry
Colville's People 2002
Emma's Dead 1992
Headstand 1990

Colville's People

Carol Malyon

The Mercury Press

Copyright © 2002 by Carol Malyon

www.colvillespeople.com

ALL RIGHTS RESERVED. No part of this book may be reproduced by any means without the prior written permission of the publisher, with the exception of brief passages in reviews. Any request for photocopying or other reprographic copying of any part of this book must be directed in writing to the Canadian Reprography Collective.

The publisher gratefully acknowledges the financial assistance of the Canada Council for the Arts, the Ontario Arts Council, and the Ontario Tax Credit Program. The publisher further acknowledges the financial support of the Government of Canada through the Department of Canadian Heritage's Book Publishing Industry Development Program (BPIDP) for our publishing activities.

Edited by Beverley Daurio
Composition and page design by Beverley Daurio
Cover painting: *Swimmer and Sun*, by Alex Colville. Used by permission.
Printed and bound in Canada
Printed on acid-free paper
1 2 3 4 5   06 05 04 03 02

Canadian Cataloguing in Publication Data

Malyon, Carol
Colville's people : poems

ISBN 1-55128-098-1
I. Colville, Alex, 1920- -- Poetry. I. Title.
PS8576.A5364C64 2002   C811'.54   C2002-904580-0
PR9199.3.M3463C64 2002

The Mercury Press
Box 672, Station P, Toronto, Ontario   Canada   M4S 2Y4
www.themercurypress.ca

in memory of ted plantos
who always read everything first

CONTENTS

I
colville's people

retrospective   13
two boys playing   14
children in tree   15
child & dog   16
labours of the months: september   17
child skipping   18
august   19
may day   20
couple on beach   21
skater   22
woman, man & boat   23
to prince edward island   24
june noon   25
headstand   26
nude & dummy   27
woman carrying canoe   28
floating woman   29
swimmer & sun   31
morning   32
sleeper   33
woman in bathtub   34
summer in town   35
milk truck   36
main street   37
man on verandah   38
looking up   39
mr. wood in april   40
in the woods   41
target pistol & man   42
church & horse   43
road work   44
moon & cow   46
crows   47

II
rousseau's jungle

overheard in a studio   51
duncan street studio   52
canvas women   53
pictograph   55
cave painting   56
illuminaysyun   57
grit   58
looking for emily carr   59
birth   62
stream in the forest   64
iris   66
old house   69
roses are red   71
four boys   72
masks   73
homage to keith haring   1958-1990   75
migratory flight   77
gershon iskowitz retrospective   79
blurred buffalo   80
untitled drawing   82
green woman   84
blue woman   86
yellow woman   87
annie's world   89
candle   coffin   eagle   cloud   91
ceci n'est pas une pipe   92
the beautiful truths   96
why is a landscape?   97
i is for island ferry   99
u is for umbrella   100
moores   101
the lynx   102
me & bride   103
rousseau's jungle   105
graffiti   107
plaster people   108
seated figure   110
helga   111
wind from the sea   113
sunset dancers   114

III
tintypes

the arrogance of photographs 117
rewind 118
hannah maynard surrealist photographer 1834-1918 120
portrait of a grandfather 121
southern ontario gothic 124
medical textbook eyes 125
tintypes 127

I
colville's people

from paintings by alex colville

retrospective

artists: their mythology
is why we need them

see how an artist curves the world
into the shape
we need to have it take

a hound swerves back   & meets
itself again   as it loops around
the patterns of a field

birds inscribe precise designs
on air   the movement of their wings
slices the sky   after they pass by
the sections of separated sky
slide back together

a cow in moonlight   a horse escaping
a churchyard gate   space curves in
upon itself   collapses   forms shapes
to fill their bony contours

tumbling together now
patterns of earth   cloud   sky
a skater's circles on ice & air
& everywhere   the contours
of a man & woman

we turn away & they embrace
like interlocking pieces of the sky

two boys playing

two boys play on a beach
& forget us

time has moulded their bodies
into the shapes of small children

there is a space
between sand & sky
that holds them

they remain
while sun fades their hair
pale as the air that surrounds them

do not look away
they cannot grow up
while we watch

children in tree

watch them if you can
hold your breath
try not to cry

there is a sky they haven't touched yet
they stretch toward it   & scamper
from limb to limb like squirrels
they lie down along a branch
& dream   watch parents
who are fastened to the ground
& cannot reach them

land unrolls below them
a patterned carpet

if they were silent
no one would know where they are

but they cannot be silent
they rustle
they are turning into leaves

child & dog

a black dog looms beside her
massive & solid

its eyes   stare through
her forehead

this child   pale   delicate

trusting the dog
& everyone who inhabits
her small world

she is so helpless
but waits   knows
she will grow into an adult
a few feet farther
from the earth

& assumes
it will make a difference

labours of the months: september

a woman was crying
in a doorway
when he left

he returns
& isn't sure
he wants to see her

perhaps she will still
call herself
mother

on the school bus
in the classroom
at recess
he tried to find her
to touch her apron
bathrobe sash
the gold ring
around her finger

behind him
the bus stands useless
took him away   was unable
to bring him back

child skipping

at recess
she watches big girls
skip double-dutch

feet dancing
as flying circles
try to catch them

she listens to them talk
they ignore boys
whose eyes are also strange

this small girl
thinks the curse means swearing

she skips alone
after school is over
practising   certain
she'll never make it

august

a girl tries to touch childhood
but her fingers are clumsy

she stands on flowers
which only seem to be static

already   as they blossom
the next stage unfolds inside them

the girl ignores flowers
& everything she knows

she stands upon a hill
& is taller than houses & buildings

it is easy to dream beyond them

she has already moved away

may day

another month
but it doesn't matter

growing older
is not the answer
to anything

how precarious
her life seems

not like the ground
she stares at
but doesn't see

how unstructured

not like the pine trees
which remember the patterns
pines have always made
against the sky

she ignores them
they do not need her

she leans against a car

somewhere else
is not an answer

couple on beach

look:

shadows are all around them
dappled in the sand

from other couples
who thought they were alone

from men who knelt
toward something

a mystery
curved against the ground

a cone-shaped sun hat
shields her from his eyes

he can taste the milk inside

skater

she balances the world
controls it
the way a frozen surface
restricts the water beneath

lines curve   & curve again
a compromise
to pressures within her
& without

she glides
too fast for us to see
how precisely
her blades slice
designs on ice

an art form   perfect
in its impermanence
as castles
a child builds on a beach

woman, man & boat

listen: silence
unfolds & surrounds her

it curves around her body
crisp as sand
elusive as water

she is inside silence
silence is inside her

a siren song
that smashes boats on rocks
& tumbles astronauts
through endless hallways

she wades into the sea
until her sturdy legs
are half-buried inside it
then hesitates
like eve

a man rides a white boat
the motor roars inside his ears

he slices toward her
stares at her white skirt
sculpted in the shape
of a seashell

he imagines
the roar of the ocean
inside that shell

to prince edward island

ask her what she watches
if she answers she will lie

she will say she looks at
earth or sea or sky
& needs binoculars
to see clearly

she hides behind them
the way astronauts   deep sea divers
radiation workers   all travellers
in alien atmospheres
are awkward inside the costumes
they wear for safety

this woman travels on this ferry
the way she travels everywhere

a man sits behind her
she knows this

june noon

a man wears a white shirt
he belongs in an office
he should not stand outside this tent
binoculars pointed toward
some horizon

a woman is naked inside the tent
green gossamer light holds her
in focus   she permits this

the man watches sky & water
there is something somewhere
he needs to understand
he uses binoculars to do this

he does not need magnification
to study the woman
who stands behind him
because he knows her completely

he is wrong

headstand

a door goes nowhere
a cat is awkward
a naked woman stands upon her head
we try to understand this
try to understand anything

beside the cat
a door goes nowhere
a woman stands upon her head
the cat ignores this
accepts whatever happens

beside her
a door goes nowhere
a cat is awkward
the woman does not care
she stands upon her head
she is calm
almost the world makes sense

nude & dummy

a woman faces a window
then glances behind her

she should not bother
to look back

at a torso
preserving one of her pasts
as though this one
is more important
than the others

a relic of an ancestor
to whoever this woman is today
irrelevant as old snapshots or letters
unchangeable as old decisions

she should discard them
keep only memories
they can be remoulded into shapes
to fit the woman she keeps becoming

look at her
she is pliant & vibrant
she holds all her pasts inside her anyway
& keeps on forming new ones

babies grow
while they're asleep
adults change into strangers
as we watch

woman carrying canoe

she balances a canoe
her head hidden inside it

she could not do this alone

water
supports her feet & ankles

light
reflects upward
lifts the canoe into blue sky

air
fills the spaces around her

grandfather
beneath the water
moves his shadow out of her way

floating woman

water is an old memory

a woman lies on water   her body sinks lower &
lower inside it   white noise of a bathing cap
murmurs against her brain

once this woman dreamed & was a bird   water
a mirage of clouds below her   a drowned
reflection of floating sky   her wings have
dwindled to silver fins   she is returning to
that old medium she once emerged from
water laps at memory synapses   slush slush
thrums against her body   lub dub

a blue ripple on the water   a curve of belly
green ripple   a curve of shin

this keeps happening

people test themselves against water   fall
inside it   glide into a world crayfish inhabit
where clams arrange themselves in patterns
that have meaning known only to clams

people float beneath the surface   sometimes
they're dead

memories slosh
against the woman's mind: grandfather tumbles
into a sludge pool   father is able
to pull him out   a girl rocks a canoe
a boy swims   but not well enough
to save her   a yellow bathing cap
bobs up & down in english bay   a stranger
watches from the shore & wonders what to do

water surrounds her   earth is a lovely dream
she just woke up from   the dream still flickers
inside her mind   the way sunlight flicks against
a green ripple of ankle   blue ripple of thigh

water is green & pink & thick & grey   pieces of
woman float on top   a slice of skull   eye socket
cheekbone   a wedge of chin   slash of torso
in blue swimsuit   curve of blue breast   blue
rib   blue belly

limbs float nearby   a hand   a knee   wedge of
left foot   perhaps the sections once fitted
belonged together   the head fastened to a body
which obeyed it

jigsaw puzzle pieces of a woman   some sections missing

water is cool as a refrigerated counter   a marble
tombstone cliff rises above her

perhaps she once was warm   loved   breathed   had friends
& family   they are elsewhere   she has abandoned them
or been abandoned

she slides lower inside the water she came from   she is
97% water   the other 3% dissolves now   she has released it
98   99   100%

someone floats inside the water   this always happens

swimmer & sun

a time when sea creatures
inhabited the world

we almost remember
those early versions
of existence

while moving backward
approaching them again

only the eyes emerge
from a world of dolphins
whales & fish

gaze straight ahead

all else obscured
hidden inside a bathing cap
or submerged within the sea

we need to believe she's human
that tides of warm salt blood
ebb & flow within her veins
that limbs glide beneath the surface
not fins   not tail

this creature of the deep
has learned the lives of seals
& plankton   seaweed   clams

we stare at each other
try to imagine
each other's world

morning

at dawn they move apart

he shaves his face
relearns its contours
to be sure of them
throughout the day

she studies a mirror
prepares an expression
to make breakfast
greet neighbours on the street

they draw edges every morning
to erase them at night

sleeper

the man lies wrapped in a dark blanket
turned away

the woman climbs out to the cold
tries not to disturb him

she climbs out to the bathroom
or the children
she sits & reads & drinks black coffee
& wonders what she's doing
then climbs back into a bed
where a man lies tangled in the bedding

she lies beside him
naked & shivering   then
tries to pull the blanket loose
to climb inside

she wants to touch him
& have him hold her
wants not to touch him
nor hear him sigh
grumble he won't be able
to fall asleep again
reminder her it's only 3 am
or 4 or 5

the woman gets up again
& drinks more coffee

the man sleeps
tangled in the bedding
so he'll know when she comes back

woman in bathtub

a woman is in a bathtub
she is vulnerable

even beneath the water
light & shadow
intrude their patterns
upon the surface of her body

perhaps she doesn't notice

she ignores the man
who stands behind her

perhaps he has a face

summer in town

a woman walks old streets
she knows now that earth is not solid

in spaces beneath her are people she loves

grandfather should create
something beautiful from wood
grandmother should bake biscuits
mother should embroider
father finally rest

but the woman needs them to hold her up

each day
her footsteps become firmer

each day
their arms crumble a little more
beneath her feet

milk truck

silence:
empty street
in a small town
early morning

men flick
milk bottles
against
that silence

it rings
& shatters
like perfect
crystal

sleepers groan
roll over
slide beneath the blankets
try to retrieve
their lost dreams

main street

this is a town
where everything
seems almost normal

women buy groceries
to grow soldiers

a soldier almost
sits inside a car
his mother almost
sees him

40 years now
since that war

her memories fading

his face blurred
indistinct
as misted windows
on a car

man on verandah

only the cat is soft
sea wall & boats & porch
are relentless as the horizon

an old man sits
on a wooden chair
& gradually sheds
all that is extraneous

see how the air each day
shaves his cheekbones a little closer

see how it combs away
more strands of hair
until his head is perfect

he ignores us   all soft things
his cat   anything beside or behind him

we see only his sharpened profile

we do not look where he is looking
dare not notice that harsh horizon
lest we begin to focus on it

looking up

limbs move slower now
& memory

thoughts drift off
& disappear

40 hours
or 40 years ago
she swirled in patterns
on this shore

an infant
throbbed inside her
relentless as
surging tide

she tilts her head back
pulls sun inside

tries to remember

mr. wood in april

watch out old man

hold onto the gothic metalwork
that twines beside you
like dead branches

the sidewalk is awkward & uneven
edges eroded   beware of hazards
beneath your feet

& yet   look up a minute
the view is worth the risk

see how the misty treetops
touch the april sky

they soften around the edges
like an old man's memory

wind blows through silent corridors
closes doors to unused rooms

this feels like april   but be careful
november prowls the street

in the woods

a man is in the woods
he wears a mask   a glove
carries a gun

there is nothing human about him
except one hand   except his eyes
these are too much
he never intended to be so vulnerable

branches are silent
they are waiting to rustle

something is holding its breath

there is danger in the woods
it wears a mask

always he has known this

target pistol & man

    : *the man*
      black sweater
      hands folded
      holding shadows
      his poster face on backwards
      eyes that saw it all
      & dreamed it into us
      through those translating hands

      dark frames
      around each window pane
      each abstract landscape
      of grey & white

      drafting table

      iron radiator
      serrated against a wall

      dark baseboard

      patterns on the tables
      & the floor

we stare everywhere
but at that gun

church & horse

squared off & true
some carpenter built
this geometric church
clapboard lined up neatly
as verses in a bible

the building is white
& angular & perfect

within   the congregation
turns prayer-book pages

they hear the horse outside
how it runs free
wild & beautiful
as it escapes the gate

listen:
they caulk the church's cracks
with loud & louder hymns

road work

a red STOP sign
wobbles on a pole

a young man stands
beside it

his yellow hat
reflects the sun
back into the sky
where it belongs

the road gang traps us
then ignores us

sweat paves narrow highways
down dusty faces of men
who pave   then pave again
earth that refuses to
be restrained

a roller moves to & fro
the road smooths out behind it
a sleek black ribbon
packaging the land

living things are being buried here
the roller hastens their
disintegration   smoothes them back
to impatient nature
waiting to reclaim them

such ecstasy now
as earth embraces them again

colours quiver a little
shiver in & out of focus

sky hums
an incessant cicada song

something is happening that
we can't understand

we are at the edge of it
holding our breath

the sound grows louder

a small cog in
earth's machinery
clicks into place

colours settle
into focus here
but still shimmer
in the distance

an old man reverses the sign to SLOW
expects us to move along
as though nothing has changed

we follow that humming sound
along a road that uncoils
into the distance

we try to catch it
speak softly to it
like a friend
sing to pretend
we're not afraid

faster & faster
distance & time unravel
like a spool
that someone dropped

moon & cow

they exist for each other
this moon   this cow

cow watches
bright dappled clouds
graze like cattle
in fields of sky

moon lightens
cow's white patches
until a cloud
lies on the ground

on a moonless night
there's no such thing as
cow

crows

only seven of them

but they hold the world
in perfect balance

between the earth & sky
their flight sustains
a tension of stark symmetry

the upthrust of their wings
supports the sky above them

their fierce downstroke
holds the earth in place

this is the reason
it is always daytime somewhere

to keep the world in perfect balance
requires a constant flight

of seven crows

II

rousseau's jungle

overheard in a studio

trust me
sculptor says to clay
trust me to touch you

let me hold you
there is a shape
you are waiting to become
i will change you
until we find it

a part
is waiting to be arm
to have hand
that can reach out
& can touch

there are parts
that would be head
or thigh or shoulder

together
let us discover
ears & mouth & eyes

it is amazing
clay can reach out now
can touch & hear & talk

move my legs a bit   says clay
help me stand up
i want to go away

sculptor tells clay
close your eyes
stay still awhile
there is something i didn't mention
this is a place that i call
kiln

duncan st studio

an artist paints two figures   a winter scene   flick of
cadmium against yellow-white   cream-white & so on   not
merely white   never that simple   pigment melted in hot wax

meanwhile   we gaze at other paintings   maybe see
the same thing the artist painted   probably not

the way we read stories   each reading a different version
staring through the coloured filter of our lives

paintings lean against each other   absorb the essence
of their neighbours   the paintings composites anyway
images superimposed   a regatta on queen street   paddlers
with streetcar & fat pigeons & pack of dogs

ghostly figures drift toward us   through layers of wax
& paint   emily carr overlaid on a bc forest   her
chickens arrayed upon her

we accept this   enjoy   don't need to understand

we walk a street   buildings surround us   & imprint on our
retinas: click click   we turn a corner   other images pile
on top   these paintings   impressions of life   that layering
palimpsest   beautiful confusion

but no   stop it   the artist finishes the winter scene   places
it upon another   upside-down onto a green tangle   summery
profusion   then presses with a hot iron   seasons blur into each
other   a daze of memory   both scenes changed forever

the way the words of a writer blend   melt into the reader's
mind & are transformed   into something more beautiful
& textured & surreal

canvas women

> *la giaconda...the most famous of all the canvas girls*
> *— eva tihanyi*

rhoda colville   mona lisa   whistler's
mother   fierce as a nun in black & white
rocking to & fro forever   wyeth's christine
on her grassy hillside   his helga   each
strand of hair separate   tinged with sunlight
if he didn't love her then what is love?
the virgin mary holding all those babies
with adult heads

they feel like family   degas ballerinas
lush renoir nudes   modigliani's
long sad faces   ancestors fastened
in faded albums   pages tattered
sepia photos coming unstuck

they exist because we need them
goya's duchess of alba   warhol's
marilyn   sargent's madame x   we feel
we own them   gauguin's dusky
tahitian beauties   exhausted prostitutes
of toulouse-lautrec   saucy cancan-dancing
jane avril

we know them   not like neighbours
who conduct the petty business of their lives
in secret   they close doors & disappear

we wander a rolling green landscape
& imagine moore's women into existence
they lie down   settle into position
arms beneath heads   legs apart   solid
serene   at peace

we are them all   voluptuous varga girls
cassatt mothers cuddling cherub children
the elegant veiled women of magritte
we wear picasso cubist faces & startle lovers
they choose a side   try to believe it

canvas women   confident   at home
inside their worlds   they represent
our complexity   if we lose them
we're incomplete

pictograph

only these marks remain
fading as we watch   gradually
obliterating   only these
& sky & sea   too late now
to ask the meaning   perhaps
it always was

a message   received in a dream
picked into rock with a sharp stone

there are so many theories: to
draw salmon to a stream   wild
animals to the hunters   to mark
events   record visions of a shaman
or young boy   alone   fasting
toward manhood

perhaps none of these   or all
it doesn't matter

we stare at circles & lines   faces
of gods or humans   fantastic creatures
seen with the third eye of the mind

we stand where that ancient stood
wait   listen   become aware   in the stillness
air & earth are alive   we hear them breathing
pulsing   lub dub   lub dub

we dare let go of our own world   travel
backward   inward   feel a spirit touch
that secret place we never mention
are too embarrassed

soul

cave painting

there was a time
between then & now
when this dying artist's work
was understood

amorphous in lantern light
it blurs in & out of focus
like a random chocolate pattern
in marble cake   or a trick
picture in a pop psychology
magazine: a young girl & an
old lady   images alternate in &
out of the concentrated eye

& our pasts
stippled with comic strip dots
too close to understand
we await old age's longer arms
in order to hold in distant focus

illuminaysyun

the dream of enlightenment   a candle
flickering in the dark cave of the mind
until we holler   *i see!   at last i see!*   or
eureka!   like archimedes

the need for a wise old woman   ancient crone
sage or medicine-man   who learned the old
stories & is able to pass them on   tongue
speaking an antique language   eyes that have
seen everything   a scarring on the brow
third-eye remnant   glowing gem stone
at the throat   we would stare   be hypnotized
but are already tranced by the eyes

to be chanting in a sweat house   dancing
the heart slowing   slipping into synchronicity
with the great pulse of the earth   a fetus
rocking in a salt sea   the mother's heart-beat
throbbing all around it   adrift in that soothing
rhythm   separate   apart   but never alone

a face appearing in the forest   indistinct
through the trees   my companions see nothing
try to pull me away   but are unable   rootlets
unfasten from my feet to grab the earth   light
shimmers   each living thing separates from
its companions   each leaf cleaves from other
leaves   becomes distinct   individual   luminous

i need to experience this too   don't hold
my hand love   this magic can only happen
when we stand   kneel   fall down   alone

         from a painting by bill bissett

grit

landscape splits apart   pulls us inside
cataclysm or slow absorption
what does it matter

this is how the world was made   keeps
being remade   how we become   earth

we fight against it   gravity   earth-pull
that power

young   strong   resisting   but finally old
exhausted   abandoned in a changing world
the unknown begins to tempt us

dinosaurs   anachronisms   we peer
around shadowed corners   consider
being dead

& it begins   we disintegrate
faster than the erosion of rock
to sand   return to the elements
we came from

rootlets absorb water   dust
blends with other dust

we are less substantial
than pottery   unglazed baked earth

degrade faster than soldiers of terracotta
buried with a chinese emperor

our grit remains

from a watercolour/gouache landscape by Holly Briesmaster

looking for emily carr

victoria:

loitering outside the house where she
was born   grew up   chattery women
in old-time dresses point out this & that
to tourists   picket fence   historic
plaque   but where is the hawthorne hedge
for three little girls to hide behind?
the cow barn & loft studio?   where is
the square-built cow?   mother?   father?
older sisters?   little dick?   three
little girls wear starched white dresses
& pinafores   clutch dolls   lop-ear rabbits
with button eyes   they play at being ladies
behind the hawthorne hedge   those little
girls: *bigger middle small*   two stayed
clean & neat   but that other   the youngest
always into mischief   her pinafore stained
by animals & dirt & life

at night   outside the rooming house on
simcoe street   house-of-all-sorts   in the old
cow pasture   trying to imagine the inside:
pulleys to hoist chairs to the ceiling
creating space   paintings   spirit talk
fastened on the walls   an easel   coffin-box
of sketches   brushes & turpentine on
top   the window black   until morning's
northern light pulls the eyes up   up
the staircase to the attic bedroom   where
totem eagles spread their wings
& cover the ceiling   beneath them
emily sleeps

a cherry tree in back garden   monkey box
for woo   apple trees   lilacs   wall-flowers
sweet alyssum   the kennels with all those
bobtail sheepdogs   punk   loo   adam
flirt   wait for emily to wake up   &
their morning run in beacon hill park

me out front on the sidewalk   listening
for bobtails   monkey   white rat   persian
cat   creaking stairtreads   the distractions
of bawling babies & fractious tenants

hearing nothing   silence

cathedral grove:

survivors   douglas firs stretch like columns
to support the sky   they have done this
for 800 years   almost forever   the grove
is dark   we sense the weight of a roof above
glance up to confirm its dark existence
then wander   explore the spaces between
columns   where scraps of sunlight slip
through that roof   dapple the ferny
forest floor

relics of the 12th century   these
giant trees simply stand here   they wait
to die   as we all do

vancouver:

inside a gallery   browsing from one
canvas to another: *mountain forest*
tree trunk   scorned as timber   beloved
of the sky   as the forest begins moving
curving   spaces appear   we enter   feel
tree trunks & branches   turn
in slow motion   entwine   pull us inside
sap & blood   our juices blend   hearts
beat to a secret primeval rhythm   roots
grab the earth   disappear deep beneath
the forest floor   we reach up   farther
farther   our branches embrace the swirling
sky   sky whirling & earth turning   we
are ancient forest creatures who can link
the earth & sky

birth

goddess splits open
mammals fish birds emerge from her body
curves of hip thigh shoulder become contours of the earth
clefts of knee elbow crotch deepen to valleys
the air is formed by her sighs
her tears create the seas

time passes & patterns happen

needlepoint/petitpoint/knit/crochet/applique/smock/silkscreen/batik
/weave/quilt/embroider/crewel/macrame/laidwork/beading/pulled-
thread/cording/couching/long-&-short-stitch/chain-stitch/satin-
stitch/split/leaf/bargello/basket-weave/raised-stem/running/
diagonal-tent/backstitch/double-cross/closed-feather/french-knot/
bullion/roumanian/hungarian/chinese-jade/scotch/single-crochet/
double-crochet/ridge-stitch/cord/wrap/brick-stitch/flame/mosaic/
crossed-corners/star/continental/josephine-knots/full-knots/
square-knots/sennets   sew onto cotton/linen/muslin/felt/batting/
pellon/fleece/canvas/18-mesh/24/48   with DMC-floss/perle-cotton/
zwicky-silk/marlitt-rayon/paternayan-yarn/then/overstitch/
overstitch/overstitch

too late now for this woman to change her mind
anyway she is strong   can do anything
hair bursts like a halo from her head
muscles contract inside her belly
she is screaming   so much pain
on & on   but she can stand it
her jaws clench
she grabs her thighs   holds them apart
forces the child out from her womb
from her vagina
its mouth searches for her breast
finds it & holds on
the woman is smiling
a new universe inside this child

or

they shave her pubic hair   is this after the enema or before?   she can't remember   her gown won't fasten   three ties are missing   anyway it only reaches to her crotch   & strangers keep peering at her crotch   poking inside it   *relax*   they tell her   *just relax*   & she tries to   her belly in spasm   her whole huge belly in one overwhelming enormous spasm   then it passes & she can breathe   but now she is screaming & someone new tells her to stop   *don't push*   they say   *relax*   they say   *just breathe*   so many strangers   who are they?   where is her husband?   where's her mother?   people keep changing   she's been here more than 24 hours   three shifts of nurses   the first ones return & say   *what? you're still here?*   they laugh & expect her to laugh too   she wants to walk but they won't let her   or squat or do anything except lie here on stiff scratchy sheets in a bed with side-rails   & scream   try not to   SCREAM   try not to SCREAM!!!   finally a stretcher   delivery room   bright lights   people   who are they?   has she ever seen them before?   they wear masks so she can't tell   her legs in cold stirrups   ether mask over her face   she feels sick   shoves it away   *push*   they tell her   *push push harder   push*   someone says   *it's a little girl*   she looks around can't see a baby   the voice says   *no   she's already gone to the nursery*   a white mask asks   *what will you call it?*   as if she cares   he pokes a needle & thread in & out   in & out   *just the episiotomy*   he says   *i'll sew it tight   make your husband happy*

from the birth project by judy chicago

stream in the forest

                                      reach

                          reach for meaning

            up

we look up
      squint
  peer through tree trunks

forget our footing

slip
        fall
                down

splat
        spatter

slide
        through green
                splotches
                          on the water

darker (down)

    darker (down)

           all
                the
                            way

            then move on
            to the next painting
            dripping   gasping
            revived

from a painting by Gustave Courbet

iris

my mother grew them
in her garden
when she had one

or she may have

this is the kind of thing
we disagree on
when she comes over for sunday dinner

i say
remember the iris
by the fence
at 14 northwood

she tells me
perhaps i'm thinking of
sweet william or
hollyhocks or phlox
& anyway
i was too young to
remember

while i suppose
she's too old to

this painting:
flowers
don't cover the canvas
but seem to

a table
mottled tablecloth
exist only to hold them

radiator   curtain   books
don't matter

only these cut flowers

& the scissors
i almost hear their
faint snip & snip

petals blur around the edges
delicate
they would disintegrate
if they were touched

fading to pastel
beside a window

beyond it must be the garden
they came from

the artist has not painted the garden
he didn't need to
i know it's there

a gaudy border
incongruous as polyester
vivid pinks & blues & yellows
purples
the green stems stiff & proud

if she didn't grow them
she should have

these blossoms change
from one kind of beauty
to another

colours fade as i watch
pale as parchment
soft as powder on her cheek

we talk of the old garden
pay close attention
to every word
search past the faces
we are wearing
for the persons we once were

i need to know
childhood happened
as i remember

she needs to be sure
how her life was

we disagree about details
& smile   trying to pretend
it doesn't matter

from a watercolour by eric freifeld

old house

details fasten this house together
the way cobwebs & dust
hold old gauze curtains

details: it hardly matters what they are
if their numbers are sufficient

curtains   a faded confusion
gathered & straight   patterned   plain
lace or solid   the arrogance of cloth
pinned up with thumbtacks
torn blind above a broken window

pillars & fretwork   support
a second floor projection   decorative
brackets below the third-storey moulding
the first floor window sills

porch floorboards
angle this way & that

old brick   its soft patina polished
until the essence of what bricks are made of
shines through   luminescent
in this half-light

each brick loses identity
fades into the pattern of bricks around it
becoming wall   each brick also
avoids this

weeds reach between pieces of pavement
connect the earth & air

people are invisible
they hide inside their rooms
old   shifting on mattress ticking
they move their belongings
from one corner to another
details gather   weight them down
hold them   crumpled
inside this house

from a watercolour by eric freifeld

roses are red

the details of their passing
survive them   & of their love
whatever their love was

memories layered upon each other
like wallpaper roses   ripped now
other patterns exposed beneath

broken mirror   plaid jacket   frypan
love-seat upholstered with roses

overturned woodstove   broken
cups   ice skate   coloured comics
opened to *the lone ranger*

colour fades
into the memory of colour

how complicated it all was
a tangle of possessions & memories
roses twined around them

the door hangs at a crazy angle
from their leaving

from a watercolour by eric freifeld

four boys

almost this could be a family portrait   old tintype   people
expressionless   posed like a cliché   but a raven perches
on a boy's shoulder   black dog peers between their legs

the oldest boy sits in the centre   youngest on the floor
between his legs   the others at either side   touching   as
though a photographer had urged them closer so they'd
fit inside his lens   it seems so natural   except...

they are wearing the same face   each one wears it like a mask

the oldest wears a shirt & tie   he hides in a small body
& pretends to be a father or a boy   they all hide inside
small bodies & assume no one will notice

their faces are old   i don't trust them   i don't trust the bird
or dog either   but believe them   these people wear masks to
distract us   they have copied us so perfectly   the knobby
hands   the long pale feet   the oldest rests his hands on the
young one's shoulders   he has seen humans do this before

there must be some reason why they are here

behind them   through the window
look   there is a pattern in the sky

from a painting by dennis geden

masks

who was that masked man?

the innocence & purity of white

cotton picked from burrs by hand
shoved in sacks   dragged along the ground
packed in bales   spun to thread
bleached   woven to fabric

a sweet young couple sleeps on white sheets
begets a family   time goes on

sheets wear thin   thrifty wife cuts them
down the middle   stitches good fabric together
tucks frayed edges under the mattress

folded at the back of a linen cupboard
when too worn for everyday use

until her husband needs them   she stitches
at the kitchen table after supper
as children struggle with homework
a tender domestic Norman Rockwell scene

in the gallery we stare at paintings
chat about them & anything else
we have learned how to do this

our minds elsewhere   shouts   terror
in the night   a flaming cross in a front yard
eyes search for clues behind a mask   ears
accommodate to words muffled by fabric

isolated inside our own masks
designer jeans   t-shirts with messages
mirror sunglasses   lip gloss
smiles painted on clowns

rangers   always alone

from paintings by Philip Guston

homage to keith haring   1958-1990

zap   zap   zap
flying saucer
to baby
zap   zap   zap
flying saucer
to this person
& that

suddenly
radiant baby
radiant this person
radiant that

they reach out
zap
touch other people
along the street
zap
spread that
radiance around
zap
they glow
dance   jump
shimmer
in bright colours

we almost forget
they're edged in
black

man with
hole in belly
john lennon

now keith's dead too

barking dog
begins to howl

no   keith hollers
just keep glowing

he shouts
from a flying saucer
dancing inside
the new york sky

migratory flight

it happens more & more often
her mind blurs out of focus without warning

the woman finishes showering
places one foot on the side of the tub
as though she will climb out

submerged in the wet mist of the room
patterns shimmer like sunlight under water
black & brown   grey & red   blue & white

machinery hums
perhaps it is only the sound
of the fluorescent light
a hum   gentle as the drone of bees
beyond a window

this is a moment so peaceful
it is a lullaby
almost lulls her to sleep

& she would sleep
but the bird is so insistent
wild & graceful
white & smooth as alabaster
its outline sharp
against the pliant intangible air
that keeps adjusting to its shape

the bird unfolds like a prelude
a beginning to the beginning
curves unfold & refold
their precise geometry of tension

fold & refold
as though to fly away forever

then hang motionless
upon the shimmered light
like a butterfly upon a leaf

the woman shudders   wonders
was it a moment or an hour ago
she began stepping from this tub?

from a painting by lawren harris

gershon iskowitz retrospective

how is it possible
for this to happen?

a youngster in auschwitz
grows up & fills a canvas
with vibrant colours:

*prisms   patterns
from a crystal teardrop*

*bright illustrations
from happy stories
painted on his mind*

*flowers   messengers
of hope   beyond a
winter window*

*fireworks
bursts of light
linger   & transform
the night-time sky*

*cells pulse to life
& multiply
at a microscope's
fine-tuning*

a post-auschwitz passion
of yellow   & blue   & red

blurred buffalo

as though we watch them from a distance of years or memory or tears

they fade in & out of the landscape of our minds   like memories we almost remember   legends we heard as children & still want to believe in

buffalo roam everywhere   on maps: buffalo new york   buffalo jump saskatchewan   in faded snapshots: tepees   the fringed jacket on buffalo bill

shaggy buffalo heads contain all the wisdom that's worth knowing

they just stand there & dream their buffalo dreams   think philosophical buffalo thoughts   they brood on history

they munch on buffalo grass & consider mathematics   wonder: if all the buffalo in the world gathered inside a field how large a space would they take?

they shit big buffalo chips that no one gathers to burn as fuel

then lift their great heads & look around   bored with each other thinking they might as well be cows   brown swiss maybe or jerseys   relaxing until milking or the butcher

they dream their hindu dreams of wandering village streets sacred   forbidden to be eaten

then wake up   remember they're only out-takes from a western movie   cluttering the cutting-room floor

or pages from a paperback by louis l'amour: mesquite sagebrush   a tenderfoot sky-lined on a hill-top apaches silent   patient   waiting   a lonesome woman fastens love-notes to tumbleweeds & lets them go

hunters wear buffalo robes   carry heavy sharps buffalo
guns   tell stories of the old days   stampedes   thousands
upon thousands   running past all day   shaking the ground
like earthquake or thunder

now the buffalo are tired   why wouldn't they be?   blurred
weighed down by history   sepia photographs   paint   melting
into a western sunset of dinosaurs   billy the kid   & all that myth

from a painting by milton jewell

untitled drawing

nine lines
vertical
interrupted by

space
a square shape
boundless
balanced
upon a
point

•

this is all that we are given

perhaps space is available so we can add
whatever we think is important:
people   or colours
textures to hold onto

lines vertical
chopped off at the bottom
by the ground   at the top
by our own limitations

this is as far up as we can look
like a painting of a forest
by emily carr

sunlight
bends through trees
so far above us
we only know
that leaves must be there

but this light:
so bright
our eyes cannot adjust
& see nothing

a window
into spaces
between bird songs

> *from a drawing by milton jewell*

green woman

green as christmas trees & holly
jealousy   traffic lights   & oz

a little misfit kid
with pale green skin & pigtails
she read *anne of green gables*
& wished anne had been happy
when she dyed her red hair green

now she dresses up & wears
jade earrings   an emerald bracelet
olive toenail polish
moss blouse   fern skirt
& chartreuse underpants

she feeds on granny smiths & salads
lime sherbet   spinach pasta
chinese tea

march 17th she pretends that she is irish
& every other day
she keeps a four-leaf clover in her wallet
whistles *greensleeves*
jogs in parks

she refuses to play monopoly
unless she can use the green vase marker
land on north carolina   pennsylvania
& buy green houses

when people asked what she'd do
when she grew up
she said   *work in a greenhouse*
plants seemed so exotic

she has more green thumbs than anyone
vines hang from ceiling hooks
screen her kitchen window
climb trellises along her bedroom walls

she mows the lawn each week
to taste that sweet grass smell
& then makes love upon it
until grass has touched her everywhere
but her grass stains never show

from a watercolour by paula latcham

blue woman

blue woman escapes the sky
tries to pretend she belongs here

scientists with fibreoptic eyes
gaze inside   at valves & chambers
of her heart   seeking defects
was she a blue baby who escaped
the surgeon's knife?   how come
she's still alive?

the woman ignores them   tries to
fasten herself to earth

she rides her lover beside blue water
beneath an empty azure sky

he opens his eyes & cannot find her

but the riding is so beautiful
he dreams he is being fucked by
the wind & sky

from a watercolour by paula latcham

yellow woman

golden sun lights up inside her
she walks in wheat fields & disappears

yellow woman   yellow hair & face
& dress   amber nipples   elbows   fingernails
& everything

strangers notice she is yellow
look away   look quickly back
unable to believe their ordinary eyes

she wears gold rings & bangles
reads the yellow pages   drinks lemonade
eats corn on the cob   egg yolks   sponge cake
hot buttered corn meal muffins

a canary sings beside her window
daffodils crowd her garden

in some schoolyard of her childhood
a youngster held a buttercup beneath her chin
& asked if she liked yellow   she had to
admit it   as yellow spilled across her neck
& dress   ponytail   plastic barrettes

this is my friend the yellow girl
her chums would say   taking her home
to show off to their parents

she studied colour charts   learned to avoid
blue men or risk green children   avoid red men
their orange babies

does her pale lover notice any more
that she is special?   does he see anything?
he gropes toward the centre of her body
not pausing to consider
how dappled shades of yellow overlap
like bits of sunshine in a painting
by a french impressionist

& her   does she notice
all the snapshots that he takes
are black & white?   in them
she could be anyone

from a watercolour by paula latcham

annie's world

her coffee table wears striped socks

not like annie who is barefoot
& holds her hands above her head

perhaps a pirouette comes any minute

she points one leg toward the
striped-sock coffee table   & it
stretches a leg too

as though they're soldiers in a parade
or dancers or majorettes

her world is blue & purple
turquoise & green   lit up by TV
& a lamp with a 25-watt bulb

she moves in a circle of light   follows
lines worn in the carpet

a snow-fence stretches from the TV
she could follow it to the blue room
discover her red spike shoes   maybe someday
she'll wear them again

the fence exists
so leaves won't cover her up

leaves balance   precarious
we applaud   this is a stage show
& annie the only actor

what does she care that she's alone?
this is her world   the world she wanted
isn't it?   isn't it?

she performs   a TV screen flickers
but she ignores it

someone said   *we all are actors anyway*
who?   she wishes she could remember

from a painting by merike lugus

candle   coffin   eagle   cloud

look around   again   again
it is the everyday which is miraculous

childhood evaporates   a door unlocks
beyond the room is everything

a forest inside a leaf
a rock floating above the sea
woman's face hidden in a veil
& all those men in bowler hats
suspended between the earth & sky

draw back the curtains
open the window
watch sky and clouds move in

try to touch
these are not fingers
that is not cloud

from paintings by rené magritte

ceci n'est pas une pipe

a painting of a pipe
is not a pipe

painted words
that say a pipe is not a pipe
are not a pipe

i touch you
pretending you are solid
& exist

& that i do
who touch you with

this hand
is not a hand

...

a man in a bowler hat is
not a man in a bowler hat

a perfect white rose
is always beside him

this is a man who
can do anything
can pretend to be
the kind of man
who would wear a bowler hat

he wakes up each morning
showers   shaves   brushes his hair
puts on a shirt   a tie   a suit
a bowler hat

goes outside   watches
other men in bowler hats
move toward him

but it doesn't matter
he is special
a white rose is beside him

sometimes the man is made of sky

. . .

they seem so innocent
inside the salmon sky

an open umbrella stands
on its handle   a glass
of water balances on top
in perfect symmetry

almost this could be
a painting of anything
an apple   a candlestick
a man in a bowler hat

but a glass of water
balances on an umbrella
this is an image
we dare not contemplate
not now   it is too late

remember when life was simple?
a child could gaze out a window
at umbrellas with glasses of water
balanced on top   & accept it
as no more strange   than rain
falling on umbrellas   on sidewalks
sliding down the window pane

this is a time we would go back to
if we knew how

we stare at this painting
try to remember

    . . .

a small table stands on an apple
a white cloth covers the table

it is enough

    . . .

this impossible vista

we fear it

black night-time silhouettes
against a daylight sky

we want to stare only at the sky
pale blue   puffball clouds
in a random pattern

or only at dark trees & houses
light shining from windows
& a streetlamp

we make excuses
the pale blue not really
a daytime sky   the scene below
not happening at night

contradiction is all around us
our existence is ridiculous

we dare not think this
placard this painting with a warning:
danger!   do not look!

from paintings by rené magritte

the beautiful truths

apple
a small table stands on an apple
a white cloth covers the table

how weak we are
we want to separate the beauty of apple
from its taste   but are unable

an apple
describe it:
green   curved   smooth

this is the shape a sphere must become
    to be of interest
a size that fits within a hand
the solid feel of it   one cannot hold an apple
   & not notice   cannot squeeze & destroy it
   like a peach
the texture of firm skin against the teeth
the taste of apple
the puckered feel of juice upon one's chin
the taste of apple
bite   then bite again
taste its tart-sweet contradiction

eve sat at this table but she is gone

we chop it into pieces   applesauce   apple
   pudding   apple pie
eat & eat until nothing's left

then sit at a table
which stands on nothing

from a painting by rené magritte

why is a landscape?

the way we fasten ourselves to the world   find
some way to live inside it   wondering
always wondering   where & who we are

trying to balance   to move   explore
inside each new set of surroundings

adjusting   calculating   orienting
against the geography of our childhood
that lodestone   compass   fastened tight
inside our minds

dead reckoning   quick   before we're dead

quick   somersault   stand on your head

which way is up?
        which way is up?
                which way is up?

perhaps this began inside the womb

a blind fetus   groping   adrift
inside the rounded inhibiting walls

reaching out   feeling the fortress give a little
rebound   rearrange itself   & shift
the earth turning   the mother restless
changing position

we are always adjusting   trying to establish
an equilibrium

having to figure it out for ouselves   ignoring
parents who tell us fairy tales & lies:
the sun rises in the east   sinks in the west
or   *at night the sun slides down to find the horizon*
& the horizon moves up to meet it half-way

fetus   child   old man or woman
peering about   reaching out
grabbing at a landscape   always changing

which way is up?
                      which way is up?
                                      WHICH   WAY   IS   UP?

for the series: what is a landscape? by mary mckenzie

i is for island ferry

this is the only way they touch the sky
this alphabet of children
anna   bernadette   charles   dimitri   eric
braced against the railing of a ferry
as wind swoops like giant birds
beneath their outstretched arms

a child lies on the ground
& watches everything: flags
that crayon their crisp shapes
against blue sky   a kaleidoscope
of t-shirts   red   green   blue
yellow   brown

he watches white birds
peck the green grass beside him
& then slide back & forth
blue sky   blue water   blue sky

he calls them birds
knowing already that he is not a bird
perhaps not yet regretting it

next year he'll call them gulls
& each year learn more & more
of what his teachers know

he learns the earth
colours will never be so bright again
as in this painted world he passes through
not yet a grown-up
no longer bird

from a painting by alan moak

u is for umbrella

grey day   grey rain
but it doesn't matter

this is just a background wash
for colours to interrupt

white & yellow rainboots
splat against the sidewalk
splash grey background paint around

children wear yellow slickers
grown-ups   pink & orange   blue & yellow
brown   carry parcels   handbags   backpacks
bright umbrellas   stripes   checks
polka dots   blue   white   red

green gingerbread houses   red stores
a deli   bright groceries
beneath an awning   stripes of
red & white

grey rain
keeps washing colours
until they're bright

from a painting by alan moak

moores

travelling thru yorkshire
on a britrail pass
gawking at the landscape of his childhood
vast brooding rocks

survivors
they emerge from from the earth
strong   triumphant   primeval
as women from childbirth
bearing their young
in their arms

they rise up   fierce
invincible

nothing can stop them
they will prevail

the lynx

ignore this cat

forget its human face
enormous
looming above us

its pointed ears
are only a legend
an exaggeration
muttered by someone
who feared it

ignore the thick paws
the body
humped above

nothing separates us from it
no zoo cage   no mesh fence

there is no protection
from its eyes

do not look into those eyes

behind it   the sky
striped grey & yellow
like the cat's eyes
we intended to ignore

avoid that sky
it is the iris of the world

from a painting by christopher pratt

me & bride

left panel: the woman
right panel: the artist who paints her
three grey panels separate them

he has pinned her like a butterfly
graceful   but awkward
hands behind her head   elbows
pointed toward us   like a set
of extra breasts

she watches us watch her
pink lipstick   pink
nipples   pink underpants

she does not watch the artist
his right fist supports a board
left hand fastens her to canvas

we consider the temperature of the room
the woman wearing only pink underpants
the artist in ordinary clothing
& a smock for protection

we want to place a shawl
around her shoulders   protect her
from the cold   the artist   our eyes
eyes of people around us
we check her body for goose bumps
& find none

then how hot & uncomfortable
the man must be   we examine his forehead
for sweat & don't find it

so this is fiction
the artist not in the right panel
but creating it   we had forgotten

suddenly we like him a little better
how perfectly he touched her
how exactly he brushed her nipples
with his paintbrush fingers

not like the artist in the right panel
his hand could have touched her
so he painted grey panels between them

we remind ourselves
this is a matter of
perspective

from a painting by christopher pratt

rousseau's jungle

a woman lies on a couch & dreams of jungles   elephant
jaguar   lion   birds adam named once   half-hidden by
branches   half-forgotten   someone charms snakes for her
his body hides inside a shadow   garments bright as birds
& flowers   music is the reason he exists   a lion watches
the woman   it has never noticed the couch before   it
wonders when she began to braid her hair   woman!   be
careful!   a lion watches!   do not look!   each eye a jewel
held by a hypnotist: count backwards to eden

. . .

a lion eats something   an animal with spotted skin   jaguar
attacks a horse   tiger attacks a buffalo   lion eats an
antelope   panther & birds wait to share it   flowers balance
high above the ground   tentative   enormous   each bright petal
perfect   they soar like opera divas   pay attention to their
lush song   ignore the ground where things kill   eat   merely
survive

. . .

a jaguar attacks a man   do not blame it   it has been
maddened by a red sun   the scent of impossible flowers
red blobs on fleshy fingers of vegetation   inside the man
red flowers wait to be exposed

...

at the last moment a buffalo brain wonders why it happens
bright food is everywhere   a tiger must be colour-blind
not to notice   bananas above them   oranges beside them on
the ground   leaves & stems surround them   green stripes
patterns of leaf & stem that layer   interlace   the whole
jungle a mesh of these green lines   a net where one animal
traps another   a buffalo eye is open   at that last moment
yellow & green & orange tangle inside that eye

...

this is how the world seems to flamingos   there are only
four flamingos left   they are trapped on the wrong side of
the river   men wait on an island to catch them if they make
it that far   water lilies are waiting   flowers stretch
high above the water   the blossoms enormous from eating
flamingos   stems thicker than flamingo necks   water seems
peaceful   but stems lurk beneath the surface to trip & tangle
awkward spindly flamingo legs   flamingos know this is an old
water-lily trick   they balance on their small strip of sand
& know it is only a matter of time

from paintings by henri rousseau

graffiti

baudelaire had a phrase for it:
the *analogie universelle*   everything
interrelated   part of an intricate
design   fragments of a universe where
all things are related   have resemblances

a white-haired woman stands alone   leans
on her cane   this empty intersection
deserted corner of new york

the similarity of patterns: designer
shopping bag   spray-painted door
everything disintegrates

the beauty of transition & decay
the texture of these old buildings
brick projections catching shadows
metal fire-escapes   jacob's ladders
rising   descending   over trash cans
& broken sidewalks

history requires a witness: she was there
& watched it happen   neighbours loved
& shouted   struggled & fucked   old folks
finally died   broken hips   alzheimer's
strokes   infants suckled   toddlers
took wobbling footsteps   grew up & then
kept walking   scattered now   a random
pattern

deserted streets   abandoned stores
newspaper windows   graffiti doors

the woman stands erect   worlds intersect

from a painting by bernard safran

plaster people

this studio: almost a hospital fracture room
an artist wraps friends & family in plaster
such trust   they let him do this   then leave
but glance back once   like lot's wife
they regret it   their arms   legs   torsos
scattered on the floor   resting
before being put to work

...

these sculptures: pale as souls or ghosts
or newborns   that innocence   vulnerability

they're busy all day long   ride buses
subways   work in cinemas   steel mills
gas stations   dry-cleaning & butcher shops

decent folk   unpretentious   obeying
traffic signals   eating at hot-dog stands
in diners   coffee shops

occasionally they surprise   balance
on tightropes   hide behind disguises

at night they long for love   peer wistful
through windows   lurk in dark hallways
outside doors   listening   needing
to understand whatever happens inside

plaster people are patient
sometimes blue

but not tonight   look outside!
they hold hands   dance in circles
perfect   luminescent
as the smiling moon

      from installations by george segal

seated figure

see this woman
how she poises on the edge of a bench
air holds & supports her

almost she forgets the earth
only one foot fastens her to it

she could stand   could fly away
air would unfold to allow it
air would hold her

but always there is the ground
that one small foot

from a sculpture by elizabeth williamson

helga

a dark hillside looms above her
solid   ominous   landscape
moves in behind   but she escapes

& wanders from light to shadow
touching the earth   rooting
to it   dizzy   holding tight
as seasons spiral on

dappled with sunlight
leaves sometimes surround her

her braids   brushed by the sun
earth tones of brown & red
green & gold   like weeds &
grasses   tendrils reach out
& interweave

the angles of her cheekbones
her limbs   strong & delicate
as branches   natural as eden
the crook of an apple tree
a crotch   where shapes in
nature   meet   merge together
& divide

she removes her loden coat
peasant dress   garland
of leaves   reveals the texture
& shadings of her skin   then
lies down   turns toward us
so we can learn the curves
& swellings of her body   pretend
we know her

she doesn't care   closes her eyes
is hidden within a dream

from a series of paintings by andrew wyeth

wind from the sea

precise brush strokes

they record how land & people
touch   define their edges

details   this is the way
we try to memorize our lives

small cracks of light
through a dark blind

lace curtains waver
by a window   light &
shadow overlap
in fragile patterns

curtains try to hold the wind
but only touch it for a moment
as it slips through
textured fingers

we remember a curtain
a blind   a window
as though we could make sense
of things   fit our past
in a design

all those images
revenants that reappear
in photographs
& dreams

from a painting by andrew wyeth

sunset dancers

sunset: see how the sky
is a stained-glass window
& the ground   & all of us who dance
our green & blue & purple dance

we tilt our faces to the sky
until they're red reflections
then turn them to the earth
making it red

the setting sun is silent
& mocks our awkwardness   shimmers
to a flattened circle   then hangs
an inch above the painted line
of the horizon   while we call
o do not go away again
we love you

sun does not trust us   as though
we only love it for its heat   its
light   *o no*   we call   *we love those things*
of course   but that's not all
we simply love you

we dance our faster dance   we chant
& call   sun never listens

from a painting by cecil youngfox

III

tintypes

the arrogance of photographs

someone pastes a snapshot in an album
or prints it on the cover of a glossy magazine
as though the image has meaning
& records what really happened

the photographer's plastic face
blink of a cyclops eye   uni-ocular vision

flick of silver & cadmium   a sudden
outline: crying child   blonde
goddess   immolated monk

we look at photos & make up stories
to go with them   fantastic   whatever
we want

the subject helpless   squashed flat
on shiny paper   words trapped
in a frozen larynx   fingers struggle
to make an invisible fist

rewind

the universe is designed to run backward or
forward   laws of physics don't contradict this

a video runs backward rewinding

autumn leaves untangle from the earth
drift upward & clutch bare branches   reds
& yellows verge to green   a paler green
then shrink to leaf buds

an old woman: her gnarled fingers press wrinkles
from her skin   she combs her fingers through her
white hair until it darkens   thickens   shines

an old man throws away a walker   then a cane
brown blotches fade from his hands   fat melts
from his belly   chest muscles expand

the woman tosses chunky oxfords in a trash bin
slips into silk stockings   shiny red shoes with
spiky heels

the couple meets   they are so beautiful
he is smiling   she is too

stop the machine!   this is the moment
they want to recapture & keep forever

but no   he plays football   sleeps through
math class   delivers newspapers each afternoon

she daydreams through high school   sings campfire
songs   plays hopscotch & skipping games   hates
kindergarten

stop it!   stop it!   stop!
quickly   back & forth
fast forward   rewind

the man & woman   where are they?

hannah maynard   surrealist photographer   1834-1918

her parlour: a shrine of children
she keeps them everywhere   in wreaths
crowns   fountains   more than 20,000
crowded into an abalone shell   she is
a pied piper   or bluebeard   of children

dieffenbachia: children flourish
on each leaf   sailor-suit boy
wide-brim-hat girls   almost buried
in potting soil

faces of dead daughters shine on
china plates   soften upon a pillow

hannah holds a skein of yarn while
hannah winds it in a ball   the wool
passes a hannah who pours tea into
another hannah's cup

hannah waits for hannah to pour her
a cup of tea   while another hannah
pours tea down on her head

a grandson sits on the floor   his bust
impaled on a pedestal above him   hannah
tips her hat to it   politely

hannah reads a book while the grandson
sits beside her   he kneels   dangles
a dead locust above her head   other
hannahs don't look surprised   they're
used to this

from photographs by hannah maynard

pictures of a grandfather

portrait, oil on canvas, unsigned, 20 x 30 inches   off-white composition frame:

an elderly gentleman   scholarly   dignified   white shirt
grey suit & tie   a book in hand   his white hair fading into
the background paint

where is the fierce black irishman people loved or feared or
hated?   the carpenter?   the sailor?   she knows he never wore
a suitcoat in his life   only an undershirt   suspenders
holding up old work pants around his bulging belly

her grandfather blazed with life   when he came home & flopped
in his mohair armchair   the world shifted   rearranged itself
around him   people paid attention

he made them feel special   in her autograph book he sketched
a schooner   wrote   *to my first mate from captain grandpa*

twice her grandmother left him   maybe because of his women
or for a dozen other reasons

such stamina   the stories: running all the way downtown
on an errand   then running back again   ten miles or more

stories of his temper: how he hated cats   once grabbed
a yowler by the tail & swung it round his head before
flinging it away

a door-to-door salesman ignored a *no-tradesmen* sign
& was tossed down the apartment stairs

sometimes she believes these stories   but not for long
of course not   not her grandfather who adored her   who
jounced her on his knee & told her stories

once she thought she saw him die

walking backward along a catwalk   towing the schooner   he
suddenly fell backward & disappeared   as though the earth had
swallowed him up   she couldn't believe it   what appeared
solid ground was really a thick black stinking sludge bed

finally he surfaced   smeared in black grease   like a
horror-movie creature

her father hosed him down   they made her promise
never to tell   in case the women made a fuss   it was
their secret   the three of them   she told no one

years later   all grown-up   she heard her father tell the story
& realized it wasn't a secret any more   maybe it never had been

she interrupted   *when he disappeared i thought he was dead*
her father stared at her   asked   *what do you know about it?*
he had written her out of his version

perhaps it made a better story   the way he'd edited her
out of his life   their family was like that

by the time her grandfather really died they no longer spoke
she hadn't seen him for half a dozen years

this oil painting: she wonders now   perhaps it was copied
from a coffin photo   why else would he agree to dressing up?

   ...

snapshot, faded, bent, taken by a child's camera, 1 1/2 x 2 1/4 inches:

a white-haired man stands on a rise of ground   from this angle
he is enormous   head thrown back   looking fierce   irascible
he wears the clothes he always wore   white undershirt   old grey
work pants held up by suspenders

he faces lake ontario where his schooner lies beneath the waves

his grandchild points the camera   she is twelve years old & stares
at that water every day   it is as endless as the sea

southern ontario gothic

snapshot: a couple stands on a roof
their children are safe beneath them

there must be some reason why they do this

they just stand there   sky-lined
arms at their sides   grant wood could
paint them   they wear their clothes
as easily as skin

old houses surround them   positioned
carefully as a stage set   gabled
windows   shaded verandahs   lush green
lawns   borders of larkspur   hollyhocks
lily of the valley   bleeding hearts

dusty relics hidden in old attics

the couple could climb down a ladder
resume their ordinary lives   walk
down a hill   enter a bright shop
& drink black coffee

graceful inside their costumes
as others are in theirs   postman
bridge-club women   old guy from
the nursing home   the waitress
with coffee waiting   marie antoinette
behind the counter who lets them eat cake

but the couple remains on the roof
outlined   stark as a metal weathervane
against the sky

they can see anything from here
they dream their dreams

medical textbook eyes

eye = i

black rectangles block out their eyes   we see only a diagnosis
elephantiasis   psoriasis   anorexia   we stare   but can't see
the people inside   can't know them   only the eyes are missing
small section of body surface   yet without them each photo is
no one

the way a corpse is not a person   *it looks just like her*
people say   not saying   *it is her*   knowing it isn't
the corpse impersonal   not a person   looks like her   but
is not   simply a container made of skin

all we see   is what we *can* see   we pretend that's all there is
peering through corrective lenses   telescopes   microscopes
still all we see is what we see

i want only those missing eyes   not the bodies
with their overwhelming symptoms   need to gaze through
those open windows & learn the people inside

overheard in childhood: *i see   said the blind man   but he
couldn't see at all*   too many sunday school classes: i confused it
with a bible story   christ placed mud on a blind man's eyes
i can see!   the blind man shouted   & for a moment he could   or
thought so   maybe it's the same thing

what did he see in that moment of belief?   was it wondrous?
worth waiting for?   ray charles stared at the sun & lost his
sight   *o ye of little faith*   jesus said   god blames people
the way people blame god   was this before or after *jesus wept?*

blind men weep too   their eyes capable of that at least
not their eyes of course but their tear ducts   *i see*   said the
blind man   just an expression   meaning   *i understand*
good for him   i see & don't

carver's story: a sighted person talks to a stranger   blind from
birth   that awkwardness   afraid of saying the wrong thing
embarrassed by the richness of his own vision   knowing he
doesn't deserve it   he tries to describe a cathedral   finally
traces flying buttresses on the blind man's hand   touching   that
communication between their worlds

& me   visiting a residence for the blind   the only sighted
person in the room   afraid of saying some wrong thing   *i see*
for instance   sipping tea   trying not   but saying it anyway
discovering they say it too   *i see*   the blind men said   &
maybe they did

tintypes

people pose   await
the stray glance of a stranger
a century later

as though they ever existed
ever held this position before

a photographer's feet
beneath a black sheet
a muffled voice
don't move   don't move   don't move

a trick   stilled life
a painting of a pipe is not a pipe

we can hold them in our hands
they stand in front of palm trees
painted on a sheet

the leaves are unreal
we try to believe in the people

or

a girl fingers a shiny snapshot
in her pocket   *here is ronnie*   she says
taking him out   passing him around
a friend takes it   says   *oooh he's cute*

somewhere
perhaps ronnie feels a stranger
brush him with her fingers

probably not

or

a painter paints a woman
& calls it *solitude*   we pretend
the woman is alone   the painter
not beside her   watching intently

she cringes from those eyes

he paints her dream of being alone

memory: pretending a memory
is true   *tell me a story*   a child asks
& the grandmother begins   *once
when you were a child*   or   *once
when you were a grown-up...*

tell me about yourself   the man asks
as though it's easy   & there is a
logical place to begin

the beginning matters
whatever she tells first
becomes most important

although she feels
whatever was most important
has already been forgotten

riddle: *i tell you this
but am a liar   what is true?*

a TV announcer: *this too is reality*

a couple takes their kids on a trip
though their friends say   *why bother?
the kids are too young   won't
remember it later*

at first they do   for months afterward
they chatter   about eating on the plane
a plastic tray   divided   like a TV dinner
paper packages of salt & pepper   plastic
forks & spoons   a wet towel in a tiny package

an alligator in the canal   a real one
not in a zoo   (an alarm clock ticks
inside a crocodile in Peter Pan)   (*how doth
the little*   chants Lewis Carroll)

sunburn   sand in swim-suits   on bedding
damp towels draped on chairs

& then the memory disappears

perhaps this is the reason for snapshots

click: a child builds a castle on the sand
years later complains   *we never do anything*
flick: a snapshot can prove him wrong

sunburn: perhaps each new sunburn is
a memory of that first one   imprinted
beneath the surface of the skin   awaiting
another summer to jog a recollection

memory: how to hold it

alzheimer's   a stroke   amnesia

someone said   forgetting
is a protection   we would go crazy
remembering everything

in the labour room the nurse says
*the birth won't come for hours
take this sedative & get some sleep*

a mother swallows a pill
not even remembering the word for no
& anyway dreaming of sleep

her son now: *no wonder*
i can't remember being born

her: *i remember enough*
for both of us

but she doesn't

memory: making up our own history
as we go along   what we remember
becomes what happened   we repeat &
repeat   needing to prove it

remember? someone begins
& the family draws closer

this is the way
families fasten themselves together
how story-telling begins

remember? asks adam
recalling suburbs

eve says   *hey sweetie*
you left out the flowering almond
& forsythia   the border
of petunias & sweet alyssum
you forgot the pink flamingos
you left out pansies

remember!   god thunders
& he tells them to write it down

credits:

two boys playing: headstand; toronto life
children in tree: poetry canada
couple on beach: quarry
woman, man and boat: poetry canada
to prince edward island: headstand; poetry canada
june noon: headstand; ars poetica
headstand: headstand; toronto life
nude & dummy: headstand; cross-canada writers' magazine
floating woman: contemporary verse 2
sleeper: contemporary verse 2
summer in town: poetry canada
milk truck: poetry canada
main street: toronto life
man on verandah: bogg
looking up: toronto life
in the woods: headstand
target pistol and man: quarry
church & horse: headstand
road work: event
moon & cow: headstand
crows: headstand; quarry, league of canadian poets poem card
overheard in a studio: headstand
cave painting: pierian spring
birth: qwerty
iris: headstand; cross-canada writers' magazine
old house: headstand
homage to keith haring: qwerty
migratory flight: headstand
blurred buffalo: arc; we all begin in a little magazine
untitled drawing: b after c
green woman: headstand
yellow woman: event
ceci n'est pas une pipe: b after c
hegel's vacation: b after c
i is for island ferry: prairie fire
me & bride: headstand
rousseau's jungle: vintage 91
graffiti: arc
seated figure: headstand; toronto life
wind from the sea: qwerty
medical textbook eyes: contemporary verse 2
tintypes: headstand

the author wishes to express sincere thanks to:

- the above journals
- the ontario arts council writers' reserve
- beverley daurio for gentle perceptive meticulous attention to these poems, and to the fragile ego of their author
- wolsak & wynn who published some of these poems in *headstand*
- and the artists: bill bissett, holly briesmaster, emily carr, judy chicago, alex colville, gustave courbet, eric freifeld, dennis geden, philip guston, keith haring, lawren harris, gershon iskowitz, milton jewell, paula latcham, merike lugus, rené magritte, mary mckenzie, alan moak, henry moore, christopher pratt, henri rousseau, bernard safran, george segal, elizabeth williamson, andrew wyeth, cecil youngfox
- information available at: www.colvillespeople.com